www.providencebooks.net

Publisher Contact

Email:contact@providencebooks.net

Social media: facebook.com/providencebooks

Acknowledgements

The team at Providence Books would like to thank our friends, family, suppliers and customers for making our vision of creating the highest-quality books a reality. Thanks for purchasing and enjoy the quotes!

This page is intentionally left blank

This page is intentionally left blank

A trifle consoles us, for a trifle distresses us.

Blaise Pascal

All human evil comes from a single cause, man's inability to sit still in a room.

Blaise Pascal

All men's miseries derive from not being able to sit in a quiet room alone.

Blaise Pascal

All of our reasoning ends in surrender to feeling.

Blaise Pascal

As men are not able to fight against death, misery, ignorance, they have taken it into their heads, in order to be happy, not to think of them at all.

Blaise Pascal

Atheism shows strength of mind, but only to a certain degree.

Blaise Pascal

Belief is a wise wager. Granted that faith cannot be proved, what harm will come to you if you gamble on its truth and it proves false? If you gain, you gain all; if you lose, you lose nothing. Wager, then, without hesitation, that He exists.

Blaise Pascal

Between us and heaven or hell there is only life, which is the frailest thing in the world.

Blaise Pascal

Can anything be stupider than that a man has the right to kill me because he lives on the other side of a river and his ruler has a quarrel with mine, though I have not quarrelled with him?

Blaise Pascal

Chance gives rise to thoughts, and chance removes them; no art can keep or acquire them.

Blaise Pascal

Concupiscence and force are the source of all our actions; concupiscence causes voluntary actions, force involuntary ones.

Blaise Pascal

Continuous eloquence wearies. Grandeur must be abandoned to be appreciated. Continuity in everything is unpleasant. Cold is agreeable, that we may get warm.

Blaise Pascal

Contradiction is not a sign of falsity, nor the lack of contradiction a sign of truth.

Blaise Pascal

Custom is our nature. What are our natural principles but principles of custom?

Blaise Pascal

Desire and force between them are responsible for all our actions; desire causes our voluntary acts, force our involuntary.

Blaise Pascal

Do you wish people to think well of you? Don't speak well of yourself.

Blaise Pascal

Earnestness is enthusiasm tempered by reason.

Blaise Pascal

Eloquence is a painting of the thoughts.

Blaise Pascal

Even those who write against fame wish for the fame of having written well, and those who read their works desire the fame of having read them.

Blaise Pascal

Evil is easy, and has infinite forms.

Blaise Pascal

Faith certainly tells us what the senses do not, but not the contrary of what they see; it is above, not against them.

Blaise Pascal

Faith embraces many truths which seem to contradict each other.

Blaise Pascal

Faith indeed tells what the senses do not tell, but not the contrary of what they see. It is above them and not contrary to them.

Blaise Pascal

Faith is different from proof; the latter is human, the former is a Gift from God.

Blaise Pascal

Few friendships would survive if each one knew what his friend says of him behind his back.

Blaise Pascal

Habit is a second nature that destroys the first. But what is nature? Why is habit not natural? I am very much afraid that nature itself is only a first habit, just as habit is a second nature.

Blaise Pascal

Happiness is neither without us nor within us. It is in God, both without us and within us.

Blaise Pascal

He that takes truth for his guide, and duty for his end, may safely trust to God's providence to lead him aright.

Blaise Pascal

Human beings must be known to be loved; but Divine beings must be loved to be known.

Blaise Pascal

I can well conceive a man without hands, feet, head. But I cannot conceive man without thought; he would be a stone or a brute.

Blaise Pascal

I have discovered that all human evil comes from this, man's being unable to sit still in a room.

Blaise Pascal

I have made this letter longer than usual, only because I have not had the time to make it shorter.

Blaise Pascal

I maintain that, if everyone knew what others said about him, there would not be four friends in the world.

Blaise Pascal

If all men knew what others say of them, there would not be four friends in the world.

Blaise Pascal

If man made himself the first object of study, he would see how incapable he is of going further. How can a part know the whole?

Blaise Pascal

If our condition were truly happy, we would not seek diversion from it in order to make ourselves happy.

Blaise Pascal

If we examine our thoughts, we shall find them always occupied with the past and the future.

Blaise Pascal

If we must not act save on a certainty, we ought not to act on religion, for it is not certain. But how many things we do on an uncertainty, sea voyages, battles!

Blaise Pascal

If you gain, you gain all. If you lose, you lose nothing. Wager then, without hesitation, that He exists.

Blaise Pascal

Imagination decides everything.

Blaise Pascal

Imagination disposes of everything; it creates beauty, justice, and happiness, which are everything in this world.

Blaise Pascal

In each action we must look beyond the action at our past, present, and future state, and at others whom it affects, and see the relations of all those things. And then we shall be very cautious.

Blaise Pascal

In faith there is enough light for those who want to believe and enough shadows to blind those who don't.

Blaise Pascal

It is good to be tired and wearied by the futile search after the true good, that we may stretch out our arms to the Redeemer.

Blaise Pascal

It is incomprehensible that God should exist, and it is incomprehensible that he should not exist.

Blaise Pascal

It is natural for the mind to believe and for the will to love; so that, for want of true objects, they must attach themselves to false.

Blaise Pascal

It is not good to be too free. It is not good to have everything one wants.

Blaise Pascal

It is the fight alone that pleases us, not the victory.

Blaise Pascal

It is the heart which perceives God and not the reason. That is what faith is: God perceived by the heart, not by the reason.

Blaise Pascal

Jesus is the God whom we can approach without pride and before whom we can humble ourselves without despair.

Blaise Pascal

Justice and power must be brought together, so that whatever is just may be powerful, and whatever is powerful may be just.

Blaise Pascal

Justice and truth are too such subtle points that our tools are too blunt to touch them accurately.

Blaise Pascal

Justice is what is established; and thus all our established laws will necessarily be regarded as just without examination, since they are established.

Blaise Pascal

Justice without force is powerless; force without justice is tyrannical.

Blaise Pascal

Kind words do not cost much. Yet they accomplish much.

Blaise Pascal

Law, without force, is impotent.

Blaise Pascal

Little things console us because little things afflict us.

Blaise Pascal

Love has reasons which reason cannot understand.

Blaise Pascal

Man is but a reed, the most feeble thing in nature, but he is a thinking reed.

Blaise Pascal

Man's greatness lies in his power of thought.

Blaise Pascal

Man's true nature being lost, everything becomes his nature; as, his true good being lost, everything becomes his good.

Blaise Pascal

Men are so necessarily mad, that not to be mad would amount to another form of madness.

Blaise Pascal

Men despise religion. They hate it and are afraid it may be true.

Blaise Pascal

Men never do evil so completely and cheerfully as when they do it from religious conviction.

Blaise Pascal

Men often take their imagination for their heart; and they believe they are converted as soon as they think of being converted.

Blaise Pascal

Nature is an infinite sphere of which the center is everywhere and the circumference nowhere.

Blaise Pascal

Noble deeds that are concealed are most esteemed.

Blaise Pascal

Nothing fortifies scepticism more than the fact that there are some who are not sceptics; if all were so, they would be wrong.

Blaise Pascal

Nothing gives rest but the sincere search for truth.

Blaise Pascal

Nothing is as approved as mediocrity, the majority has established it and it fixes it fangs on whatever gets beyond it either way.

Blaise Pascal

Nothing is so intolerable to man as being fully at rest, without a passion, without business, without entertainment, without care.

Blaise Pascal

One must know oneself. If this does not serve to discover truth, it at least serves as a rule of life and there is nothing better.

Blaise Pascal

Our nature consists in motion; complete rest is death.

Blaise Pascal

Our soul is cast into a body, where it finds number, time, dimension. Thereupon it reasons, and calls this nature necessity, and can believe nothing else.

Blaise Pascal

People are generally better persuaded by the reasons which they have themselves discovered than by those which have come in to the mind of others.

Blaise Pascal

People are usually more convinced by reasons they discovered themselves than by those found by others.

Blaise Pascal

Reason commands us far more imperiously than a master; for in disobeying the one we are unfortunate, and in disobeying the other we are fools.

Blaise Pascal

Since we cannot know all that there is to be known about anything, we ought to know a little about everything.

Blaise Pascal

Small minds are concerned with the extraordinary, great minds with the ordinary.

Blaise Pascal

That we must love one God only is a thing so evident that it does not require miracles to prove it.

Blaise Pascal

The charm of fame is so great that we like every object to which it is attached, even death.

Blaise Pascal

The consciousness of the falsity of present pleasures, and the ignorance of the vanity of absent pleasures, cause inconstancy.

Blaise Pascal

The eternal silence of these infinite spaces frightens me.

Blaise Pascal

The finite is annihilated in the presence of the infinite, and becomes a pure nothing. So our spirit before God, so our justice before divine justice.

Blaise Pascal

The gospel to me is simply irresistible.

Blaise Pascal

The greater intellect one has, the more originality one finds in men. Ordinary persons find no difference between men.

Blaise Pascal

The greatness of man is great in that he knows himself to be wretched. A tree does not know itself to be wretched.

Blaise Pascal

The heart has its reasons of which reason knows nothing.

Blaise Pascal

The immortality of the soul is a matter which is of so great consequence to us and which touches us so profoundly that we must have lost all feeling to be indifferent about it.

Blaise Pascal

The knowledge of God is very far from the love of Him.

Blaise Pascal

The last act is bloody, however pleasant all the rest of the play is: a little earth is thrown at last upon our head, and that is the end forever.

Blaise Pascal

The last proceeding of reason is to recognize that there is an infinity of things which are beyond it. There is nothing so conformable to reason as this disavowal of reason.

Blaise Pascal

The least movement is of importance to all nature. The entire ocean is affected by a pebble.

Blaise Pascal

The only shame is to have none.

Blaise Pascal

The present letter is a very long one, simply because I had no leisure to make it shorter.

Blaise Pascal

The self is hateful.

Blaise Pascal

The sensitivity of men to small matters, and their indifference to great ones, indicates a strange inversion.

Blaise Pascal

The strength of a man's virtue should not be measured by his special exertions, but by his habitual acts.

Blaise Pascal

The struggle alone pleases us, not the victory.

Blaise Pascal

The supreme function of reason is to show man that some things are beyond reason.

Blaise Pascal

The weather and my mood have little connection. I have my foggy and my fine days within me; my prosperity or misfortune has little to do with the matter.

Blaise Pascal

There are only two kinds of men: the righteous who think they are sinners and the sinners who think they are righteous.

Blaise Pascal

There are some who speak well and write badly. For the place and the audience warm them, and draw from their minds more than they think of without that warmth.

Blaise Pascal

There are two kinds of people one can call reasonable: those who serve God with all their heart because they know him, and those who seek him with all their heart because they do not know him.

Blaise Pascal

There is a God shaped vacuum in the heart of every man which cannot be filled by any created thing, but only by God, the Creator, made known through Jesus.

Blaise Pascal

Through space the universe encompasses and swallows me up like an atom; through thought I comprehend the world.

Blaise Pascal

Thus so wretched is man that he would weary even without any cause for weariness... and so frivolous is he that, though full of a thousand reasons for weariness, the least thing, such as playing billiards or hitting a ball, is sufficient enough to amuse him.

Blaise Pascal

Time heals griefs and quarrels, for we change and are no longer the same persons. Neither the offender nor the offended are any more themselves.

Blaise Pascal

To have no time for philosophy is to be a true philosopher.

Blaise Pascal

Too much and too little wine. Give him none, he cannot find truth; give him too much, the same.

Blaise Pascal

Truly it is an evil to be full of faults; but it is a still greater evil to be full of them and to be unwilling to recognize them, since that is to add the further fault of a voluntary illusion.

Blaise Pascal

Truth is so obscure in these times, and falsehood so established, that, unless we love the truth, we cannot know it.

Blaise Pascal

Two things control men's nature, instinct and experience.

Blaise Pascal

Vanity is but the surface.

Blaise Pascal

Vanity of science. Knowledge of physical science will not console me for ignorance of morality in time of affliction, but knowledge of morality will always console me for ignorance of physical science.

Blaise Pascal

We are only falsehood, duplicity, contradiction; we both conceal and disguise ourselves from ourselves.

Blaise Pascal

We conceal it from ourselves in vain - we must always love something. In those matters seemingly removed from love, the feeling is secretly to be found, and man cannot possibly live for a moment without it.

Blaise Pascal

We know the truth, not only by the reason, but also by the heart.

Blaise Pascal

We like security: we like the pope to be infallible in matters of faith, and grave doctors to be so in moral questions so that we can feel reassured.

Blaise Pascal

We never love a person, but only qualities.

Blaise Pascal

We only consult the ear because the heart is wanting.

Blaise Pascal

We run carelessly to the precipice, after we have put something before us to prevent us seeing it.

Blaise Pascal

We sail within a vast sphere, ever drifting in uncertainty, driven from end to end.

Blaise Pascal

We view things not only from different sides, but with different eyes; we have no wish to find them alike.

Blaise Pascal

When we are in love we seem to ourselves quite different from what we were before.

Blaise Pascal

When we see a natural style, we are astonished and charmed; for we expected to see an author, and we find a person.

Blaise Pascal

Words differently arranged have a different meaning, and meanings differently arranged have different effects.

Blaise Pascal

You always admire what you really don't understand.

Blaise Pascal

This page is intentionally left blank

This page is intentionally left blank

This page is intentionally left blank

This page is intentionally left blank

This page is intentionally left blank

www.ingramcontent.com/pod-product-compliance
Lightning Source LLC
Chambersburg PA
CBHW061939280526
45787CB00004B/1660